Biology –
"The Human Body"
Anatomy

NON-FICTION

FeB 12 1973

MAR. 5 1973

JAN. 28 1974

MAR 1 1 1974

MAY 8 1974

C

WHAT'S INSIDE OF ME?

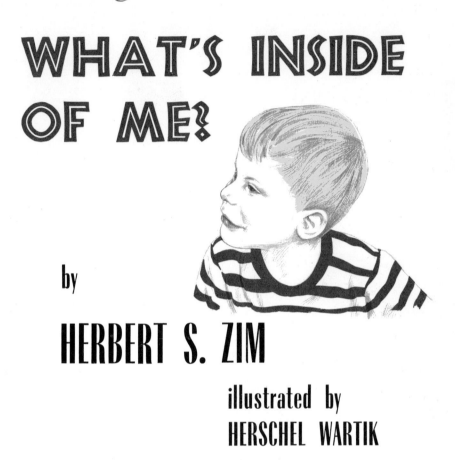

by

HERBERT S. ZIM

illustrated by
HERSCHEL WARTIK

WILLIAM MORROW & COMPANY
New York   1952

Foreword

This book will help young people to understand their bodies. The youngest can discover facts from the pictures alone. Those who are older will find further help in the captions and in the large-type text. The more detailed text, in smaller type, is for adults who are using the book with children and for young people who are better readers.

Grateful recognition is given to Frederic R. Steggerda, Professor of Physiology, University of Illinois, for checking the manuscript and illustrations.

WHAT'S INSIDE OF ME?

Beneath the skin and muscle that cover your body are many parts called organs. These fit and work together like parts of an auto or radio. Each organ does its own work and each helps the other. Some organs are large; some are small. Each is made of tiny parts called cells. Here are a few of the organs that are inside of you. Some of the others are behind this front layer.

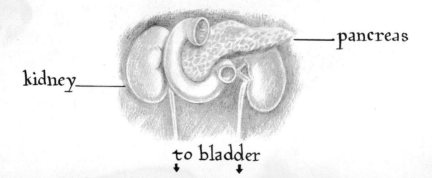

kidney_____   _____pancreas

to bladder

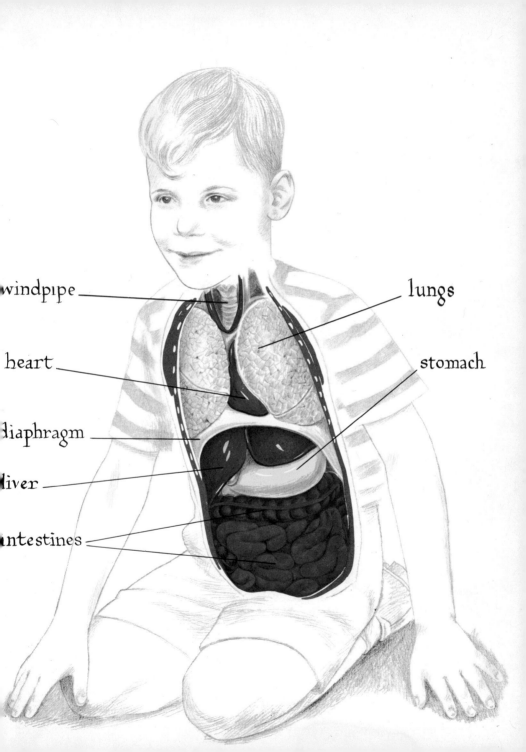

windpipe

lungs

heart

stomach

diaphragm

liver

intestines

You are alive because all the organs of your body work together. Your windpipe connects your throat to a pair of lungs made of millions of tiny bags or air sacs. The air you breathe is mostly made of gases called nitrogen and oxygen. The nitrogen is of no use to you; the oxygen is. In your lungs, the oxygen from the air passes into your blood. Each minute you take in about a cupful of oxygen. Your heart pumps blood, with food and oxygen in it, to every part of your body. Your heart lies in the middle of your chest between your lungs. A thin sheet of muscle called the diaphragm separates the heart and lungs in your chest from other organs lower down in your abdomen.

Most of the organs in your abdomen take care of food. Beginning at your mouth, the food you eat moves through a tube over 30 feet long. Its first stop is in your stomach. There the food is mixed and you begin to digest it. When food is digested, it changes and becomes something like a thin soup.

Most food is digested in the long, twisting intestine which begins at your stomach. From here it passes into your blood and is ready for your body to use. Your liver and other organs pour juices into the intestine to help digest the food. The liver also stores up some of this digested food, keeping it ready to pour into your blood whenever you need it. By the time food has passed through the intestine, all that could be digested has gone into your blood. What is left is waste. When you move your bowels, you get rid of this waste.

WHAT'S INSIDE MY HEAD?

There are seven openings in your head. Your mouth is the top end of the food tube. The two openings of your nose lead to a tube that goes to your throat. This nose tube joins your throat near the windpipe, which goes to your lungs. Your two eyes and two ears connect to your brain, the most important organ in your head. Your skull is made of small, flat bones. Eight of them cover and protect your brain. The other fourteen are the bones of your face.

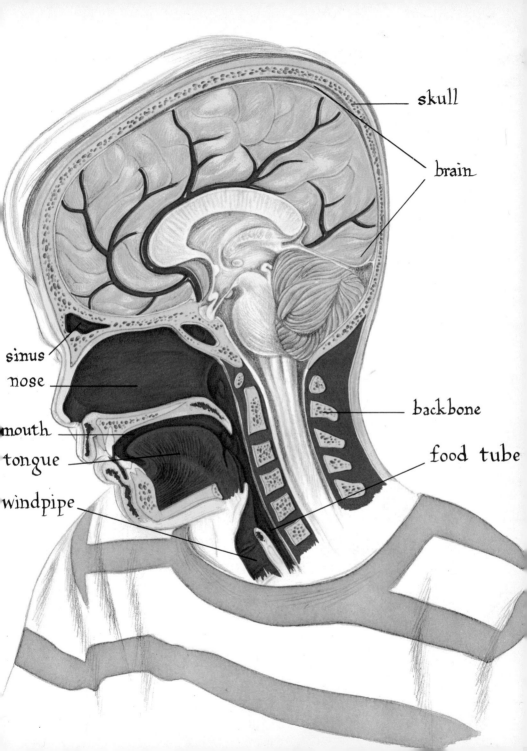

skull

brain

sinus

nose

mouth

tongue

windpipe

backbone

food tube

Your head has two parts: your face and your brain. The head of a dog or cat is mostly face. The brain takes up only a small part. Your brain is larger and takes up more than half your head. Eyes, nose, mouth, and ears make up most of your face. Your eyes are like cameras taking colored pictures of everything you see. The picture is in your brain. Your brain makes you know what you have seen. Your nose is a passage for the air you breathe. Smells are picked up by your nose, and a message is sent to your brain. Your brain may then tell you what you are smelling.

In your mouth are teeth to chop and grind food. By the time you were about two years old you had your first set of teeth. After a while, these first 20 teeth fall out, one at a time, and you get new teeth which should last all your life. A grown person has 32 teeth. The tasting spots on your tongue are called taste buds. They work only when your tongue is wet. Dry your tongue with a towel and have someone put a bit of salt or sugar on it. Can you taste now? At the back of the mouth, the nose tube joins your throat. Tiny tubes from the ears join here, too. Just below is the voice box, where air from your lungs moves past your vocal cords to make sounds when you talk or sing.

Each person's face is a bit different from that of everyone else. Some people have wider noses, thicker lips, or bigger ears. But each part of every head, inside and out, does the same work for each of us.

WHAT'S INSIDE MY BRAIN?

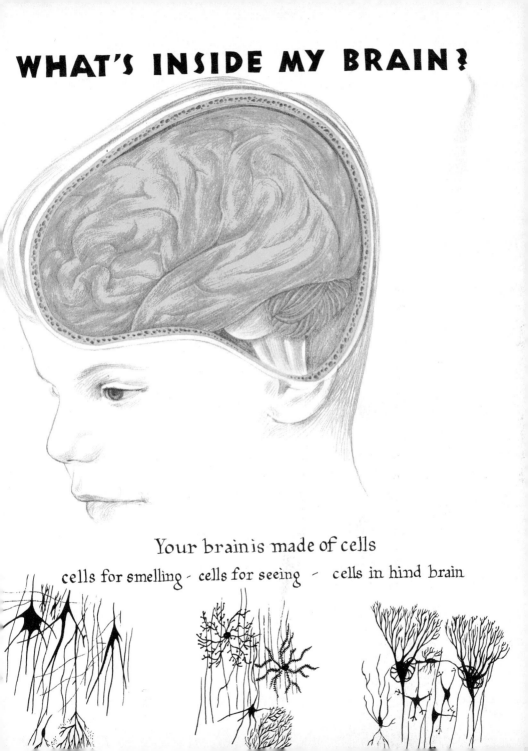

Your brain is made of cells

cells for smelling - cells for seeing - cells in hind brain

For your size you have a large brain. So has every human being. But the size of your brain is not as important as the wonderful way it works. Your brain is made of millions and millions of cells. These are so small they can be seen only by using a microscope. Yet each is alive and helps you think, feel, and do things. Some cells in your brain are long and thin, like tiny wires. These carry messages, as tiny electric currents, from one part of the brain to another.

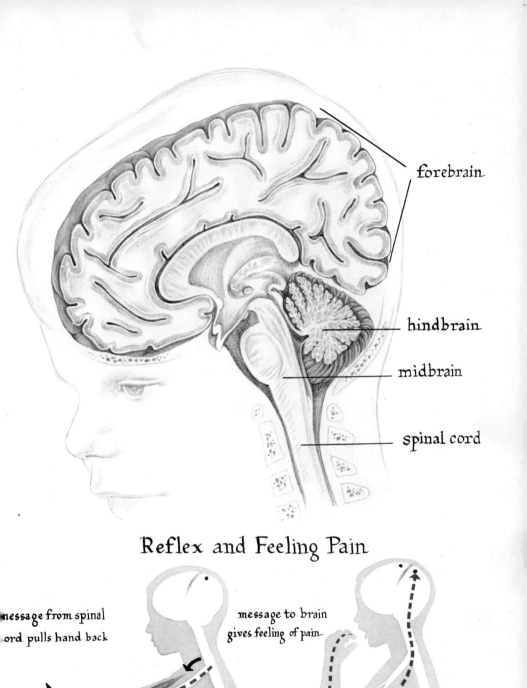

forebrain

hindbrain

midbrain

spinal cord

Reflex and Feeling Pain

message from spinal
cord pulls hand back

message to brain
gives feeling of pain

People are wiser and can do more things than other animals because of their wonderful brains. We can talk, read, write, build houses, and invent things. Your brain has three main parts: the front brain, the hind brain, and the middle brain.

The front brain is the largest. It is gray outside and white inside. This is the part of the brain where you remember, think, and plan. With this part of your brain you make your arms and legs do what you want them to do. Here is where the messages from the eyes, ears, and nose let you see, hear, and smell. The hind brain is smaller than the front brain and is more like that of other animals. This part of the brain gives you balance and control of your muscles. You walk without tripping and skip without falling, because the hind brain is doing its job. If it were not, you would lose your balance and fall over.

The middle brain is the smallest of all, but very important. It controls the beating of your heart, swallowing food, breathing, and other things you do without thinking. The middle brain is a small swelling where the brain joins the spinal cord—a large bundle of nerves in your backbone. The spinal cord is the main road to and from the brain. It comes into the middle brain bringing messages from all parts of your body. It also takes charge when some part of your body is in danger. If you touch a hot iron, the message to the spinal cord makes you pull your finger away even before you feel the pain of the burn. This is called a reflex. Nerves connect most parts of your body to the spinal cord.

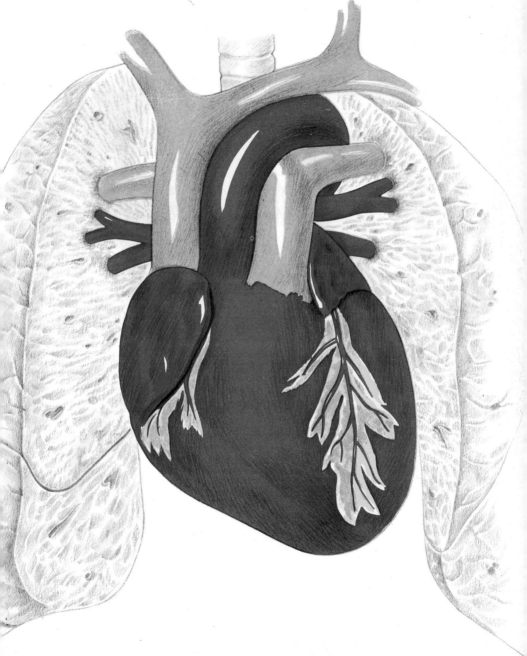

Your heart beats all your life, all the time, day and night. With each beat it pumps blood through living pipes, or blood vessels, to every part of your body. The blood vessels near your heart are large. They branch, getting smaller and smaller on their way to the cells of your arms, legs, and head. Blood takes food and oxygen to all the cells of your body. Other blood vessels, first small, then larger and larger, bring blood back to your heart.

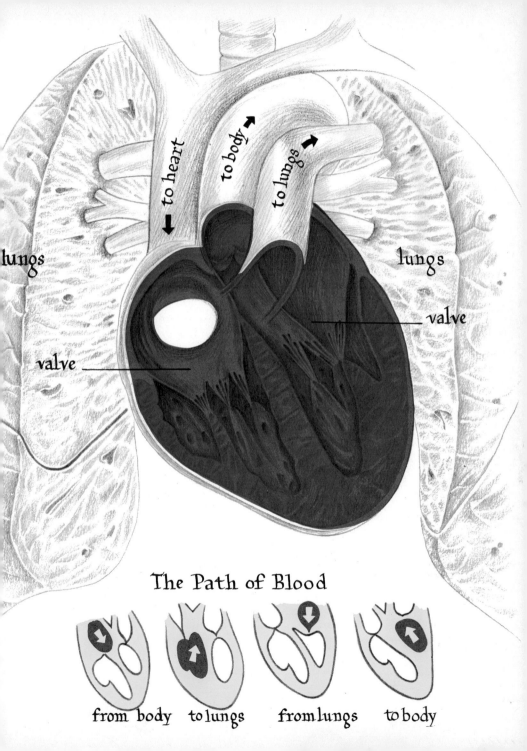

to heart

to body

to lungs

lungs

lungs

valve

valve

The Path of Blood

from body   to lungs   from lungs   to body

Your heart is a hollow ball of muscle about as big as your fist. When you are grown up, it will weigh about half a pound. It started beating very fast before you were born. When you were born it was beating about 140 times a minute. As you grow older, it beats slower and slower. A grown person's heart beats 60 or 70 times a minute. When you are resting, your heart beats slowly. Your body does not need as much food and oxygen then. When you are running and playing, your heart works more and beats faster, pumping blood to the muscles of your arms, legs, and all the other parts of your body.

Your heart has four parts, or chambers. Blood comes into your heart through the top two, from your lungs and other parts of your body. The bottom two chambers are larger and have stronger muscles. They pump blood from your heart to your lungs, stomach, arms, liver, and every other part of you. The chambers pump, one right after the other, so the blood is always on the move. Between chambers, and where the blood leaves the heart, are valves which open and close. Each valve is a flap. After each heartbeat, the valves keep the blood from moving backward. With each beat of your heart, blood is sent through your blood vessels. If you put your hand over your heart or on the pulse in your wrist, you can feel each pumping message as your heart beats. When a doctor listens to your heart, he can tell whether or not the valves are working as they should.

WHAT'S INSIDE MY STOMACH ?

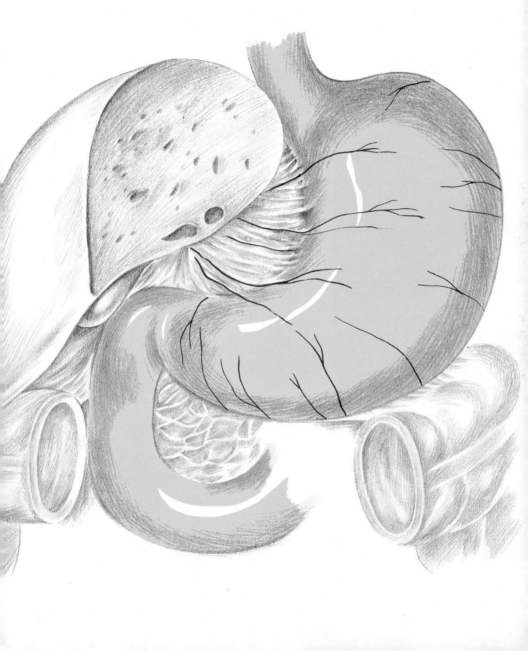

Your stomach is an enlarged part of the long food tube. It is a bag with walls of muscle. Food comes in through an opening at the top. In your stomach, the food you have eaten is mixed with juices made by the lining of the stomach. These help digest some of the food. Foods like bread or sweets do not stay in your stomach long. Meats, cheese, and milk stay longer, and fatty foods stay the longest. From the stomach, the food moves into the intestines.

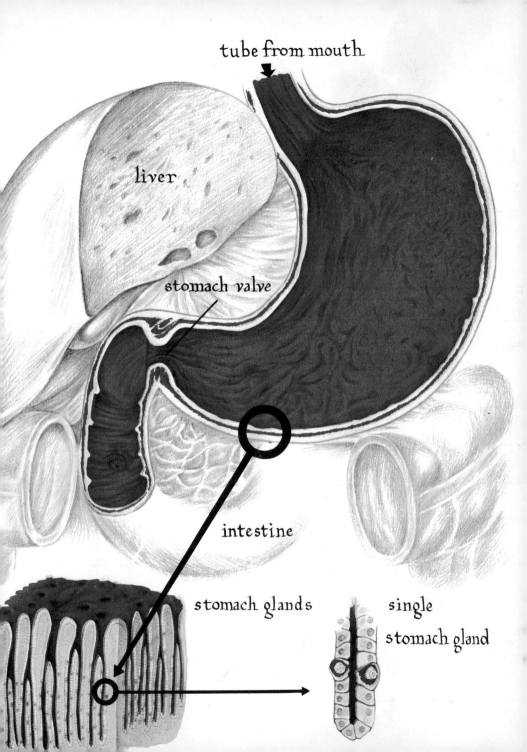

tube from mouth

liver

stomach valve

intestine

stomach glands

single
stomach gland

Even while you are chewing your food, you begin to digest it. The saliva in your mouth starts to change part of the food, so it can later pass into your blood. The glands in your mouth make over a quart of saliva every day. Saliva mixes with food as you chew, and by the time food reaches your stomach, saliva has begun to digest part of it.

Your stomach is a bag of muscle that stretches as you fill it with food. A grown person's stomach can hold over a quart of food. A child's can hold less. The stomach muscles squeeze, churn, and mix the food. While they are doing this, glands in the lining of the stomach make juices which digest the food. There are many, many glands in the lining of the stomach. Each is a long, tiny tube lined with dozens of cells. These cells are different from brain cells or muscle cells. Their job is to make stomach juices, and that is all they do. They make over a quart every day. The food you eat, mixed with saliva and stomach juices, changes and becomes more and more like watery soup.

When the food is well mixed and partly digested, a valve at the lower opening of the stomach opens, and the food moves on into the intestine. This is a long, narrow coiled tube about four or five times as long as you are tall. More food is digested in the intestine than in the stomach. Here, juices from the liver and other juices mix with the food. Each kind of juice digests a special type of food. The digested food soaks through the walls of the intestine and passes into the blood. Then the blood carries it to all the parts of your body.

WHAT'S INSIDE MY SKIN ?

The cells of your skin have pigment which gives your skin its color. Everyone has the same kinds of pigment in his skin. But some skins have more of one pigment. A Negro's skin has more dark pigment.

The skin that covers your body is partly alive and partly dead. The outside layer of skin, the one you touch, is dead. The live cells of the skin are on the inside. These cells are pushed out as new cells grow below them. The skin cells die as they are pushed out. They join the layer of dead cells that cover and protect the living cells below. Dead skin cells rub off all the time. Oil glands keep your skin soft. Sweat glands help cool your skin.

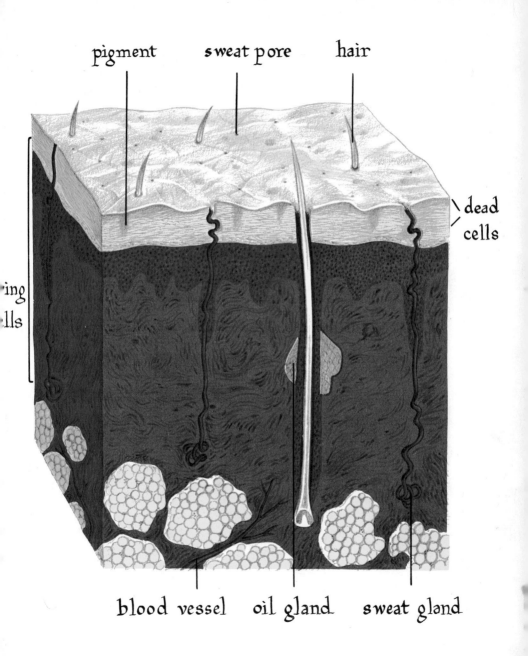

pigment   sweat pore   hair

dead cells

ʾing lls

blood vessel   oil gland   sweat gland

Your skin does several jobs for you. It protects your body against heat and cold, and against disease. Germs cannot enter the body through a healthy skin. They can get in through a cut or an opening. Whenever you cut yourself, be sure to put medicine on the cut right away in order to kill germs.

Your skin helps keep your body cool. The sweat glands in your skin are always making sweat, which is mostly water. This helps cool your skin. When you are hotter, you sweat more. You may even see drops of sweat on your skin. But even if you cannot see the sweat, you are sweating all the time. You sweat a pint of water a day, and more when it is warm. Besides water, sweat contains a small amount of waste which your body gets rid of as you sweat.

Your skin does other work. Your hair grows from it. Hairs are dead, but they grow from living cells. Your fingernails and toenails also grow from living cells in your skin. Like your hair, they are dead. Your skin makes oils which keep it from drying and cracking.

In your skin are nerve cells. Some nerve cells in your skin give you the feeling of heat or cold. Some give you the feeling of pain. Some give you the sense of touch. The nerves in your skin join other nerves that carry messages to your spinal cord and so to your brain. Some parts of your skin are ten times as thick as other parts, but all parts are made up of the same layers of cells.

WHAT'S MY
SKELETON LIKE?

Your bones give your body its shape and form. They make it possible for you to stand, run, jump, and lift things. Bones protect and cover important parts of your body like your brain, heart, and lungs. Bones are alive and growing. They grow fastest when you are young. Eating meats, eggs, cheese, and beans gives your body the stuff to build bones. Every year you may grow two or even three inches taller, till you reach your full height.

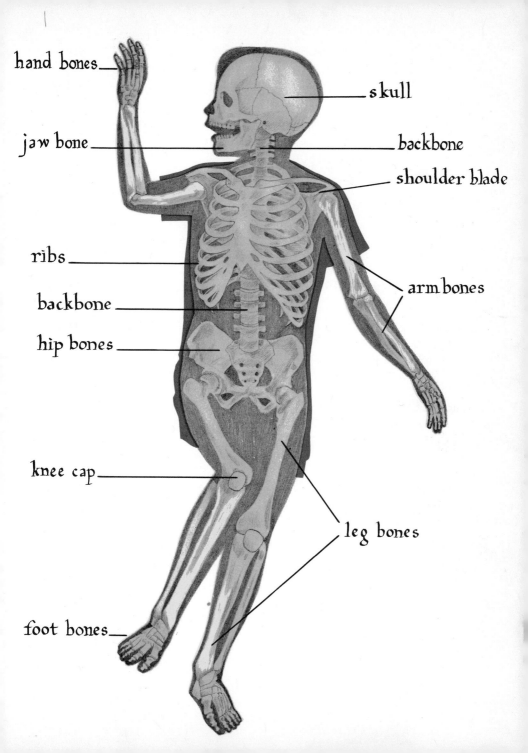

hand bones

skull

jaw bone

backbone

shoulder blade

ribs

backbone

arm bones

hip bones

knee cap

leg bones

foot bones

Your skeleton is made up of about 200 bones. Some are very small, like the bones in your ears. Others are large, like the bones in the upper part of your legs and arms. In your arms there are 64 bones; in your legs, 62. Most of these bones, and bones like your ribs, are called long bones, even though some are only an inch or so long. Long bones are hollow, and soft at the ends. The inside is filled with soft yellowish or reddish marrow. It is in the red marrow that red blood cells are made. Next time you eat chicken, look at the drumstick. It is very much like the long bones of your arms and legs. It is hard at the middle and soft at the ends. If you break it, you will see it is hollow.

Your backbone is made of about 20 small bones that fit closely together. The spinal cord that connects so many nerves to your brain runs through the backbone. The bones that form the lower end of your backbone grow together as you grow older. Nine bones join together till they look like two. Your 24 ribs and your breastbone form a basket which holds and protects your heart and lungs. Your curved hipbones help hold up your intestine and other organs in your abdomen.

Your skull rests and turns on the top bone of your backbone. In your skull itself there is only one bone you can move—your lower jaw. Put your fingers in front of each ear and feel the ends of the jawbone move as you chew. Your teeth are not made of bone. They are made of much harder material.

This is your arm. You can
see some of the bones and
larger muscles. When you bend

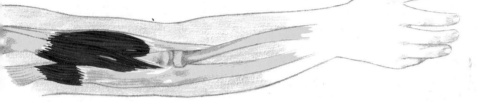

your arm, some muscles stretch
while others shorten. Both sets
work together to make your
arm move. When you move
your arm, nearly all the other
parts of your body help you
to do so.

When you bend your arm, you do so for a reason. Perhaps a fly has landed on your nose and you want to brush it away. That means you know the fly is there. You feel it tickling your nose as it moves. Already your eyes and the skin of your nose have sent messages to your brain. Now you know what is happening. Quick as a flash, you know without thinking what you want to do, and more messages go out from your brain through the spinal cord and nerves to the muscles in your arm.

But you don't want to bend your arm any old way. So other parts of your brain take care that there is just the right amount of bending. As you brush away the fly, your hand moves over the tip of your nose and does not punch you in the eye by accident.

All these parts of your body have worked together in less than a second, to do something you wanted done.

Your brain and nerves and muscles could not do their work without food and oxygen. Your lungs do their share by taking oxygen out of the air you breathe and moving it into your blood. Food that you have digested and stored in your body gets into the blood also. Your heart keeps the blood moving, so that the food and oxygen are carried to every cell that needs them. All these parts and many others, working together, make you able to do the many things you want to do. You can run, play, and make things, because the parts of your body work together even better than the parts in an auto or in a radio.